IMAGES
of America

MOUNT PLEASANT
THE VICTORIAN VILLAGE

IMAGES
of America

MOUNT PLEASANT
THE VICTORIAN VILLAGE

Mary-Julia C. Royall

First published 1997
Copyright © Mary-Julia C. Royall, 1997

ISBN 0-7524-0531-4

Published by Arcadia Publishing,
an imprint of the Chalford Publishing Corporation
One Washington Center, Dover, New Hampshire 03820
Printed in Great Britain

Library of Congress Cataloging-in-Publication Data applied for

Contents

Acknowledgments		6
Introduction		7
1.	The Front Beach	9
2.	The Municipality	21
3.	Medicine in the Village	35
4.	Churches and Cemeteries	41
5.	Education in the Village	51
6.	Activities on Shem Creek	61
7.	Ferries, Trolleys, and Buses	67
8.	Children	73
9.	Recreation	93
10.	Growth Begins	119

Acknowledgments

To portray what the place and the people were like in this earlier, more leisurely paced time, representative pictures, stories, and reminiscences have been chosen from the abundance so freely shared by those who still remember the Village. Many had to be omitted, due to space limitations.

Appreciation is extended to all the many friends and family who have participated in this project, in particular the following, who shared information and photographs from their collections: Gertrude King Appleby, Robert Legare Coleman, the City of Charleston City Hall Collection, Betty Wacker Douty, the descendants of Drs. J.Y. DuPré and E.M. Royall, Eliese Tiencken Farmer, Marie Mellichamp Gleaton, Sarah Royall Hamlin, Barbara Magwood Hedgepeth, A.L. Lofton, Henry Mellichamp, Sarah McIver Townsend, and Effie Leland Wilder. The author supplied many of her own photographs in addition to copying all the submitted images. Thanks go to Exposure 60 for processing the film. A particular thank you to Lou Edens of the Museum on the Common and the Shem Creek Maritime Museum and to Don Embrey of the Town Planning Staff, and most of all to my husband, Jervey D. Royall.

Books and booklets used include *Christ Church* (1961) by Anne King Gregorie, *History of Mount Pleasant* (1960, 1970) by Petrona Royall McIver, Minutes of the Christ Church Parish History Club by McIver (secretary 1927–1933), *Laing School 1866–1926* and *South Carolina Electric and Gas Company, 1846–1964* by Pogue, miscellaneous booklets, various newspaper articles, and postcards. Appreciation goes to Mayor Cheryll Woods-Flowers for permission to use the Town of Mount Pleasant booklets, maps, and historic district survey, as well as their photocopying facilities. The Waterworks dedication booklet of 1935 also provided valuable information

The book is dedicated to the memory of Petrona Royall McIver, who almost fifty years ago inspired my love for the history of the area.

Introduction

Across the harbor from Charleston, the Town of Mount Pleasant has always had its own identity. Developing basically at the same time as the city, it is not the typical bedroom community of suburban living. It had its genesis as small English villages located on the water's edge which eventually merged and formed the Town of Mount Pleasant.

With the rapid growth of the second half of the twentieth century, the ambiance of the small town, lovingly referred to as the Village, is fast disappearing. This pictorial history records what life was like in the earlier part of this century before World War II in the area along the harbor, the historic district.

The unique character of this waterfront area has been recognized and in 1973 it was placed on the National Register of Historic Places. This 30-block area is bounded on the north by Shem Creek, on the east by the western edge of Whilden Street and Royall Avenue (with the exception of the lot on the east side of the street containing St. Andrew's Episcopal Church), on the south by McCants Drive, and on the west by Charleston harbor.

The book is divided into general sections. Overlapping will appear because it is difficult to categorize a community. It is not a chronological nor comprehensive study of the history of the area. It is simply a view of times past as recorded in photographs. For detailed information the reader is referred to McIver's *History of Mount Pleasant*.

Themes developed include the geographical front beach area, the municipality with public buildings and businesses, doctors and druggists, churches and cemeteries, the Academy and Laing schools, activities on Shem Creek, ferries, trolleys, and buses, children, and recreation. The last part will focus on events which made possible the rapid expansion of the area—the opening of the Cooper River bridge in 1929 and the 1935 completion of the waterworks system for the town. The centennial of the 1837 incorporation was celebrated. Pictures taken at this performance conclude the story of the Village.

A brief account of the original little settlements along the waterfront—the Ferry Tract, Greenwich Village, the Village of Mount Pleasant, Hilliardsville, and Lucasville—will help explain the unique character of this part of the Town of Mount Pleasant.

THE FERRY TRACT. In 1770 Andrew Hibben obtained from the government a charter for what was the first ferry service directly connecting the Mount Pleasant area with the City of Charleston. A few houses were already located on the Ferry Tract, which adjoined Mount Pleasant Plantation (owned by Jacob Motte, the Charleston City Treasurer) and Hibben's land on Shem Creek.

In the eighteenth century taverns were the equivalent of today's motels. They were located at strategic intervals along the King's Highway, an important northern route, later known as the Georgetown Road (now Highway 17). Here travelers could find food and lodging for themselves and their horses. Scott's tavern was the hostelry nearest Shem Creek.

Two contemporary references to Scott's are interesting. William Hort, an early settler from Barbados, wrote in his diary that in 1775 his daughter, Elizabeth Haddrell Hort, was born in

Jonathan Scott's house, Haddrell's Point, in Christ Church Parish. Originally Haddrell's Point Plantation, owned by George Haddrell, encompassed most of the area from Shem Creek over to Center Street and up to Highway 703 and 526, almost 500 acres.

Another reference to Scott's was in a letter written on Christmas Eve 1775 by Thomas Pinckney to his sister Harriett. His military group from Charleston had landed near Motte's Plantation, then "marched to attack some chocolate and sausages well supported by cherry bounce and plain brandy at Jonathan Scott's." The soldiers needed food!

GREENWICH. In addition to the tavern, Jonathan Scott owned other property, including a mill on Shem Creek and a 100-acre tract between Mount Pleasant Plantation and the land of William Hort. The Englishman called both his mill and his subdivision Greenwich.

Begun before the Revolution about 1766, Greenwich was the first little village in the area. Fifty acres were divided into building lots. The streets were named Pitt, King, and Queen. The street on the harbor was called Bay. Greenwich Common on the other 50 acres provided a place where citizens could graze their livestock and procure firewood. Years later, in 1889, an Act of the General Assembly made it legal for the Common to be surveyed, divided into building lots, and sold.

MOUNT PLEASANT. In 1803 Andrew Hibben's son James bought Mount Pleasant Plantation from the estate of Jacob Motte. In 1808 he had John Diamond survey and divide the 78 acres into thirty-five building lots, thus creating the Village of Mount Pleasant. His will, probated in 1835, names which lots are willed to his nine surviving children. Tradition says he gave lots to the churches and school. Although not shown on the 1808 plat, nor mentioned in his will, the 1838 plat of the 1837 Incorporation shows certain lots marked for these purposes.

Streets composing the Village of Mount Pleasant were named for families—Bennett, Whilden, and Venning. Hibben Street was the boundary between the Village and the Ferry Tract, which James Hibben also owned. Beach Street along the shore was indeed a sandy beach.

HILLIARDSVILLE. In 1847 Charles Jugnot and Oliver Hilliard began a development which they called Hilliardsville. The streets were Division (now McCants), Center, and Middle. Development now extended along the waterfront from Shem Creek to the cove by Sullivan's Island.

The developers provided building lots and established an entertainment park which they named Alhambra. To make the lots salable, they installed a drainage system. To get customers for the bowling building and the octagonal dance hall, they ran a ferry from Charleston which docked at nearby Ferry Street. Located on the waterfront area of William Hort's extensive property, the park included Hort's Grove, long a popular picnic area. The magnificent oaks still stand. Hilliardsville became a part of the town in 1858.

LUCASVILLE. The remaining village to become part of Mount Pleasant was Lucasville. Developed in 1853 on land owned by Jonathan Lucas' son William, it was bounded by Shem Creek and Bennett, Hibben, and Boundary (now Simmons) Streets, and was originally a part of the Ferry Tract. Both Lucasville and the Ferry Tract joined the town in 1872.

It is hoped that, through this sketch of how the town developed, a better understanding of the place and its people can be gained. The orderly development of the area produced a cohesiveness that remains today.

One
The Front Beach

The National Register Historic District of Mount Pleasant includes the area of the original settlements. The waterfront part has long been called the front beach. Originally it was a hard sand beach which was used as a street, but as tidal action was slowed by stone jetties near Alhambra, marsh covered the sand. The land of the East Cooper area is geologically classified as the Wando-type soil, not the type found on island beaches and dunes.

Although there were year-round residents, Mount Pleasant was a summer resort from early times. Planters came down from their plantations to find a healthier climate, and people from Charleston came over on ferries to their summer cottages.

Houses were built with the climate in mind. Cross ventilation would catch any prevailing breeze. Exterior blinds shielded against the sun and the rain. Houses were built high off the ground to escape the low-flying insects, and they faced the water, which was the primary mode of travel early on.

The beauty of the Village shoreline was uninterrupted. Short docks allowed the owners access to the water from their houses as the tide came in.

Pictures of some of the houses on the waterfront illustrate how the Village grew. Others show activities on the front beach.

In laying out the Village of Mount Pleasant for James Hibben in 1808, John Diamond created thirty-five lots; of these, six were on the waterfront with #1 belonging to James. No pictures have been located of either Andrew Hibben (17?–1784), the silversmith from England who married Elizabeth (Barksdale) Wingood (a widow with a good inheritance), or of his son James (1766–1835), the founder of the Village of Mount Pleasant. Pictures of James Hibben Jr. (b. 1799) and his wife, Rebecca Stiles, are characteristic of the era. James Jr. had been willed Lot #6, which was located next to Greenwich Village, on the water.

The Hibben family was prominent in civic and government affairs. James was a representative and senator, and one of the incorporators of the Academy in 1809. He also raised and equipped a company of cavalry volunteers in the War of 1812. James Jr. served as aide-de-camp to Governor Thomas Bennett as well as serving in the House of Representatives. His sister Martha had married the brother of the governor. Her father's will gave her Lots #8 on Bennett Street and 20–24 on Whilden Street. The Hibben family formed the nucleus of the newly formed village.

James Hibben's house was on Lot #1 which extended from the water to Bennett Street. A peach orchard is noted on the corner. Currently seven lots are located on this Hibben Street property. Probably the house was constructed around 1754 following the devastating 1752 hurricane which covered the area with 17-foot tides. It was a typical farmhouse with four rooms downstairs and two up. About one hundred years ago the owner, R.H. Pinckney, enlarged it to a full two stories and added the columns.

The front of the house faced the water according to custom. The second-story porch is a recent addition. The bluff, some 20 feet high overlooking Charleston harbor, was the site of both Revolutionary War and Confederate forts as shown on contemporary maps and by artifacts found here.

Kitchens were separate buildings because of the danger of fire. Their chimneys were massive compared to the size of the building because cooking was done over the open fire with the iron pots suspended on hooks that could be swung in and out.

The house could not have had a more sympathetic tenant than the William Whilden McIver family. They purchased it in 1912 and became the longest owners of the property. Both were descended from early local families. Petrona Royall McIver (1883–1973), a great granddaughter of Sarah Margaret Hibben and Daniel DuPré, had grown up in the house next door. In 1960 her love of local history resulted in the printing of the *History of Mount Pleasant*, sponsored by the Town. Mayor Francis F. Coleman had approached her about a brochure; the result was a definitive account of the town. Ten years later she completely revised it when Mayor G. Magrath Darby requested it be reprinted as a contribution to the South Carolina Tricentennial.

Many events have taken place here during the past 250 years. During the Revolution, there was an exchange of letters between General William Moultrie and Lord Montague in which the General, a prisoner of war, refused to accept a commission and desert the patriot cause, as he wrote from Haddrell's Point, March 12, 1781. In 1758 Chief Justice Charles Pinckney, ill with malaria, was brought to the more healthy area of the Village to recuperate. However, he died on July 12, in this house.

A copy of the Moultrie-Montague letters was presented to the house in 1931 by the Moultrie Memorial Association of Charleston. In 1936 a bronze marker was placed over the door by the Rebecca Motte Chapter of the Daughters of the American Revolution. This festive occasion included the band from Fort Moultrie and notable speakers. Also shown in the picture are the lion's head from the bow of a shipwreck found on Long Island, and the running light from the ferry *Lawrence*.

The Leland House, Lot #2, was built about 1820. Aaron Whitney Leland (1787–1871) of Massachusetts graduated from Williams College in 1808 and came to Mount Pleasant to be a tutor in James Hibben's family. In 1809 he married James' oldest daughter Eliza (1792–1856). He was headmaster of the newly chartered Academy in 1809. After some years as a teacher he became a Presbyterian minister, serving First (Scots) church in Charleston and then on James Island. He later became professor of theology at the Columbia Theological Seminary. Of their five sons, three became physicians and two became teachers. Their four daughters all married Presbyterian ministers.

The house on Lot #2 bears some resemblance to the Hibben house, where Eliza lived with her parents and siblings. The lot is a particularly large one extending 487 feet north, 437 feet south, 250 feet east, and 259 feet west.

In 1815 Sarah Margaret Hibben (1795–1843), the second daughter of James, married Daniel DuPré (1793–1878). Her father gave her lot #3. Daniel inherited an estate on the Santee River which made him independent. He worked with the Methodist church, and preached at the Wappetaw Independent Church, at the Huguenot Church in Charleston, and then at St. James, Santee. A member of the House of Representatives, he was a signer of the Ordinance of Secession. Daniel and Sarah Margaret had nine children. One, Ann Allston, married John Adams Leland, "the boy next door."

His house was probably constructed about 1820, and part of it seems to be in the present structure. It is another house several stories high, with a porch on the prevailing breeze side, a design usual in the early town.

The Venning family was another early family in the area. Samuel Venning was one of the town commissioners in 1837. His lot in Greenwich was adjacent to Mount Pleasant Village. Another Venning, Mortimer, also lived in Greenwich on Lot #5 at the foot of King Street c. 1860. Robert Murrell Venning and his son John are pictured. His lot, #6 at the end of Mount Pleasant Village, had been willed in 1835 to James Hibben Jr., who moved to Massachusetts.

His home, still standing on Bennett Street, was another house built in the typical style of two stories with porches facing the water. Nicholas Venning lived at the end of Venning Street on Lot #4. His home is seen in many of the waterfront photographs.

Short simple docks were constructed on the front beach where locally made boats were tied up. Within half an hour after the tide started coming in, there would be enough water to float the boat and rowing away to the chosen fishing drop could be accomplished. One of the best fishing areas was a certain place in the harbor which lined up with "Miss Dolly's bay window." Although she was a portly lady, it is assumed the window on the house at the end of Venning Street is what is meant. It was built in the early 1800s on Lot #4 and owned by Nicholas Venning.

How wonderful for children when the weather turned warm and they could take off their heavy winter stockings and go down to the water's edge and go wading. "Miss Dolly's" house is to the right. Inside the harbor the water was calm and there were no dangerous holes. It was safe for youngsters.

17

Called the "Beach House" by the family that built it, this home is located on the Ferry Tract. Facing the harbor, it was designed to catch any breath of air. The owner was a planter, Thomas J. Hamlin.

The toddler, a grandchild, is on her way from the Beach House down the "Boulevard" to the water's edge, about 1919. Trolleys may be seen on the Hibben Street Ferry wharf.

The McKinley house, dating from about 1878, no longer stands. It was located in Hilliardsville, where Pierates Cruze homes are. Looking toward the city, you can see the ferry wharfs. After the Dana Osgoods purchased it in 1928, they developed Pierates Cruze Gardens on the property. Azaleas and camellias added beauty, but most spectacular was the panoramic view of the harbor.

Staying in her own yard, this little miss finds plenty to play with. Imagination is wonderful.

This shoreline view from Hilliardsville looking toward Greenwich includes the light keeper's wharf. Lights and buoys in the harbor were manually controlled, and the government provided housing at the end of Bank Street. The federal government purchased the property in 1857 and probably built the house and wharf soon thereafter. In 1946 it was sold since mechanization had taken over.

A canoe ride when the sun was setting was a peaceful way to end the day. The Hibben Street Ferry wharf is on the right. Charleston is in the background.

Two
The Municipality

A live oak tree is an appropriate symbol in the logo of the town. Throughout its history, mention was made of the lovely groves of oaks in different parts of the Village. Those mentioned in Hort's Grove of the early nineteenth century are probably the ones still standing in Alhambra Park.

A contemporary account describing the new Presbyterian church on the outskirts of the Village referred to it as being in a lovely grove of oaks.

Near the Darby building is a massive oak on the edge of Pitt Street, while around the corner others are found near the Confederate Cemetery. Throughout the Village are many others.

The Town's motto means "We Grow," certainly an apt designation.

This chapter includes a brief mention of two mayors, various town-related buildings, organizations, and businesses.

Intendant Elias Whilden's family came to Carolina from Massachusetts in the seventeenth century. After the little villages of Greenwich and Mount Pleasant were incorporated, the town was governed by an intendant (mayor). There was also an official clerk who kept the records. Elias Whilden was one of the early intendants, serving from 1857 to 1858. Of the four commissioners who laid out the town, he and Andrew Hibben (son of James) lived in Mount Pleasant, while Joshua Toomer and Samuel Venning were in Greenwich.

Elias Whilden's home, built c. 1825, was on Lot #9, at 236 Bennett Street. Elias had two daughters and five sons. One of his children, John Marshall, called the "Boy Major," died in the second Battle of Manassas. Johnnie's four brothers also served the Confederacy.

The Robert V. Royall family is shown here in 1896. Mayor Robert Venning Royall served sixteen years, the longest of any mayor, from 1898 to 1914. He was the son of Dr. E.M. Royall and Anne Bailey Venning. His wife, Sallie, was the granddaughter of the Reverend Daniel and Sarah Margaret (Hibben) DuPré. In addition to serving as mayor, Robert was a teacher, a principal of Charleston High School, and a surveyor. This image was made from a glass negative. Notice the family cats were also included in the picture.

The house was next door to the Hibben house on part of Lot #1. When their youngest daughter was a baby the family left the McClellanville area and moved to Mount Pleasant. During the time he was mayor trees were planted along the streets.

One of the buildings that has served as a town hall is this small structure. Probably constructed about 1890, it has been moved from its original site on Pitt Street over to Royall, and now is on Bank Street in Edwards Park, where it serves as a branch police station.

Built in 1884 as the Berkeley County Courthouse, the Darby Building has been used for many purposes. When Moncks Corner became the county seat of Berkeley County in 1895, this building was used for a short time as a school, then a seminary, next as a church, and for a short time as the town hall. It is now used by the recreation department of the town. When used as a courthouse, offices called the Law Range were used by county officials. The *Berkeley Gazette*, a weekly newspaper, was published here. Firsthand accounts cataloged the damage of the 1886 Earthquake. The editor, Yates Snowden, became a professor at the University of South Carolina. Another weekly, *The State Gazette*, had a short run from 1913 to 1914. Its first issue contained a history of the Village written by a recent graduate, Martha McCants.

Although Mount Pleasant was on the direct mail route from the north, citizens had to watch the Charleston newspaper for their name to appear in the "advertised letter list," and then go to the city to pick it up. By 1875, mail was coming to the Village. Several individuals served as postmasters, using their homes or other nearby buildings. Around the turn of the century, the Patjens family built a little office adjacent to their store on Church Street and Rivers Lane. This small building, used until 1917, is now located on the corner of Bank and Pitt Streets in Edwards Park. Various original memorabilia has been given to or bought by the Alhambra Garden Club, which has charge of the building.

As the Village grew, more room was needed and a larger wooden structure was built on Pitt Street in the business district. This served until 1946, when the post office was moved across the street to a brick building. The post office served as a gathering place for the citizens when it was time for the mail to be put into the boxes.

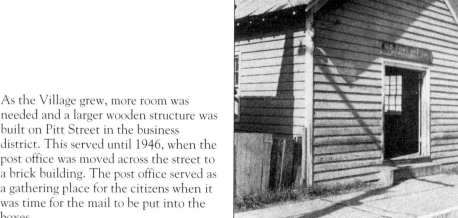

Alhambra Hall and Park encompass Hort's Grove on the harbor, an early picnicking place. Massive oaks still stand in the area. When Jugnot and Hilliard purchased part of the property in 1847, they designed a park with swings under the oaks and an octagonal building which they named Alhambra that was used for dances. There was even a bowling building. To encourage people to use their facility, they ran a ferry from Charleston to the foot of newly formed Ferry Street.

The present building was constructed in 1937 using timbers from the abandoned Hog Island Ferry building located near the foot of the Cooper River Bridge. The Town owns the property and sponsors events such as the Childrens Festival and the Blessing of the Fleet. The hall is used for social events such as weddings and receptions, which have to be scheduled well in advance.

The Mount Pleasant Yacht Club had its headquarters at Alhambra for many years. Reorganized in 1933, the *Essolene* was their entry in the regatta the following year. The regatta began with a dance at the former Hog Island Ferry terminal, followed the next night by a dance at the Isle of Palms, and the finale was a street dance on Pitt Street, which was ablaze with festoons of lights and gay with bunting. The next year the *Nell* was the contender. Then the old ferry building was dismantled and timbers from it used to build the present Alhambra Hall.

The Christ Church Parish Agricultural Society was composed of planters, many of whom lived in the Village. This group picture probably represents a joint meeting with societies from other areas. Posters on the wall at the left would be to demonstrate the latest techniques in farming. The Society building on Highway 17 still stands and is used as a residence.

Etiwan Lodge No. 95 A.F.M. was constituted in 1859. For two years the members met in the town hall. Then for $500 they purchased the 1835 chapel that had been moved from the corner when St. Andrew's Episcopal Church was built. Before the "war of invasion," as their secretary termed it, they prospered; they had lecturers, and ministered to the sick and the bereaved. Times were so hard after the war that dues could not be paid and had to be cancelled. However, on St. John's Day, June 24, 1869, they met as a body and went to the Ferry Wharf to meet the Grand Lodge of South Carolina for a celebration. This is still an active body of Masons. The King's Daughter's Hall across Whilden Street from the Masonic Lodge is no longer in existence. It provided a place for performances and had a lending library.

Fund-raising for construction of Christ Church Lodge No. 44 of the Knights of Pythias included picnics at Alhambra. Built in the late 1800s, it burned around 1914. It was quite a large structure near the beach on the south side of King Street. Upstairs contained a kitchen, pantry, stage, and dressing rooms. Downstairs held offices, a kitchen, and a dining room which opened on to a large piazza. In addition to lodge activities, traveling shows put on performances here.

For many years the business district of the Village was located in the area of Pitt from Morrison to Venning Streets and the nearby block of Church over to Whilden Street. Looking south, stores on Pitt Street included the post office, a grocery, and Dr. Wacker's drug store. Across Pitt Street was the Academy.

Pitt Street is shown here in a view looking north. The scene is little changed although it is some years later and the street has been paved. Oyster shell was used for paving, hence the term "shell roads." The foundations of the Revolutionary War barracks near Rifle Range Road, made of tabby (oyster shell), were used for road building.

Lunden's Store was at the end of Pitt Street, and fronted on Venning. It is now an apartment building. It was one of the numerous stores built and operated by the Germans who settled in Mount Pleasant around the middle of the last century. On the left is another store of the same background which has been adapted to the changing times and is now Guilds Inn.

When Pitt Street was to be extended to Shem Creek, a grape arbor stood in the way whose owner defiantly refused to allow its demolition. Therefore the street could not be straight. Since the Presbyterian church had recently been built on the next corner, the new street was named Church as it continues to the Creek. The scene on the postcard shows Patjens' store on the east side of Church Street and other stores nearer Venning.

J.H. Patjens' grocery store was another rectangular building three stories high. The store was on the ground level and the family lived upstairs, as was the custom. Mr. Patjens also had a livery stable. During World War II the store was made into apartments. It is no longer standing.

1865   **SEVENTY YEARS OF**   1935
SERVICE

Established in 1865, J. H. Patjens & Son, Mt. Pleasant's Oldest Continuous Business, extends its 70th anniversary greetings to the people of Mt. Pleasant and our visitors

J. H. PATJENS & SON

Staple and Fancy Groceries

Mt. Pleasant, S. C.

The 1935 booklet prepared for the dedication of the Waterworks System contained much information in the form of articles. The advertisements also prove enlightening. Here Mr. Patjens states his is the oldest continuous business in the Village, having been started in 1865.

This bakery, on the corner of Whilden Street and Rivers Lane, was another of the German-owned stores. The Wittschen family ran a bakery, as did the Moessners. The building has been converted into apartments.

N. Albergamo had a store on the corner of Pitt and King Streets. He was from Italy, as were the Megnas, who had a store on the opposite corner. In the 1935 booklet Albergamo advertised as the Star Mercantile Co., carrying general merchandise, and also as the Carolina Fish and Shrimp Co., wholesale distributors of large ocean prawn and fish. His store has become a residence.

What became a successful enterprise began when "Miss Edna" Sassard took some of her homemade relishes across Church Street to be sold at Patjens' store. Now orders come from all across the United States as the business is continued by her family in the building behind their house which children call the "pickle factory." Labels for her products were printed by her husband, "Mr. Billy," in his print shop, with the motto "Made its way by the way its made." Consternation arose when he printed some for another lady which were too similar to "Miss Edna's."

Sweet grass baskets made just north of the Village found their way into many homes. Not only was the product useful, but friendship with the maker was valued. Maggie Mazyck represents one of the "old timers" who brought baskets, flowers, and produce to her customers. Her sewing basket, made in the early 1930s, was on exhibition at the American Craft Museum, N.Y.C., in 1995. The fragrant grass grew only in certain places, and was pulled, not cut. When dried, it was made into useful items by sewing the strands with palmetto heart which had been torn into narrow strips. Sometimes pine needles decorated the basket. This truly beautiful craft is unique to the area. Mention should be made of the door-to-door vendors with the produce from their little farms. Measuring was not done by scales but with containers—such as a quart of butterbeans. Shrimp was sold by the plate (about a pound and a half).

Service stations increased with the opening in 1929 of the Grace Memorial Bridge over the Cooper River. Stations of the various oil companies were built. In the mid-1930s the Sinclair agency had this station, full service, as was the custom. Run by the Douty family, it was located on Highway 17 at the bend where Whilden joins Coleman. Just up the highway was Darby Brothers Garage for general auto repairing.

The First Tourist Court (motel) in Mount Pleasant was built adjacent to the Sinclair Station. By comparison with the elegant ones of today, it was quite primitive. Tourists had to use the restroom facilities at the service station.

Three
Medicine in the Village

The diagnosis and treatment of disease was not well defined in the era between 1860 and the 1930s. Infant mortality was high and childhood diseases took their toll.

Although the geographical situation of the Village made it an unlikely location for yellow fever to occur, it did strike with particular violence in 1857. There were some forty-one cases with eleven deaths, all within two months in a community of 1,200. It was not until the turn of the century that the carrier was determined to be the mosquito.

During the War between the States, there were four hospitals in Mount Pleasant, or Haddrell's, as it was also called. The Methodist and the Presbyterian churches were used. The Post Hospital was under the supervision of Brigade Surgeon Matthew S. Moore. He had charge of the area from Sullivan's Island to the North Carolina line, with his headquarters here.

Dr. Moore wrote on November 21, 1864, a thank you letter to Mrs. Mary A. Snowden for donating some gin and various foodstuffs, including forty-seven chickens in coops. "My own experience is that good feeding, good nursing, gentle stimulation and kind words and attentions from the doctor will cure more cases in Military practice than physic."

House calls were made with the aid of a horse-drawn buggy even after the turn of the century. Two nineteenth and two twentieth-century physicians and a druggist will be highlighted in this chapter.

Although the parish had been served by physicians since the 1700s, some of whom came from London, two locally educated physicians practiced here before the turn of the century. Both Doctors Edward Manly Royall (shown here) and John Young DuPré were born in 1827, and both served as surgeons in the Confederacy. Returning home Dr. DuPré settled in the Village; Dr. Royall on his plantation Palmetto Grove (now the site of Palmetto Islands County Park and adjoining subdivision) where he became a planter as well. In his more rural practice, Dr. Royall contracted yellow fever in 1878 but recovered.

Eventually Dr. Royall moved to the Village to a home his son-in-law had built for him at 121 Live Oak Drive, where he died in 1915 at the age of eighty-eight. His wife, Anne Bailey Venning, died in 1920.

Dr. DuPré was the son of the Reverend Daniel DuPré and his wife, Sarah Margaret Hibben, whose home was on Lot #3 of Mount Pleasant Village. John DuPré noted in one of his medical books that he resumed his practice of medicine on March 22, 1869. He, his wife, and her sister died within a week in the influenza epidemic of 1900.

Dr. DuPré's home formerly stood at the corner of Bennett and Hibben Streets. It was originally built by his uncle, Andrew Hibben (son of James, the founder of the town), who deeded it to him on March 30, 1867. His daughter and her family later lived there for many years.

Dr. DuPré's office stood in the corner of his yard facing Bennett Street. Patients came and rang the bell at the gate for him to come and attend their needs. House calls were also a part of his practice. A tax receipt noted that he paid $2 for having a horse.

Payment for services rendered was not always in money. This picture made by a patient for him was possibly all the remuneration he received. A tribute expressing the high esteem that was afforded him came in the form of a quilt made by the ladies of the Earnest Workers of the Presbyterian Church and other friends and presented to him in 1895. Each had embroidered her initials somewhere in the square she designed of silk and satin pieces. Now on display in the County Library on Mathis Ferry Road, it is a wonderful illustration of the sense of community the people of the Village shared with their "beloved physician."

Dr. James Frampton and Dr. W.J. Bowen practiced about the same time during the early part of the twentieth century. No picture is available of Dr. Bowen. He lived at 312 Venning Street in the Queen Anne-style two-story house. He, too, had a separate office building in the yard. The story is told that even after he bought his first automobile in 1912, he kept his horse and buggy. Dr. Bowen, a staunch Methodist, died in 1938. His son Boone became a professor at the Candler School of Theology, Emory University. Dr. Frampton, like Dr. DuPré, was an elder in the Presbyterian Church.

Dr. Frampton's home and office was at 310 Bennett Street. The story is told that during one of the terrible storms, time came for a baby to be delivered. The military band from Fort Moultrie had taken refuge in that very house, as it was the custom for people from the islands to come to higher ground in Mount Pleasant and stay wherever they could find room. As the wind howled outside, the band played downstairs, the baby arrived upstairs, ushered into this world by Dr. Frampton, who then had to make his way home over downed picket fences along the three blocks which he traversed like a ladder on his hands and knees.

Doctors frequently had on hand the usual medications which they prescribed for their patients. Porcher's *Plants of the Field and Forest* was a standard reference book. Using a mortar and pestle, they knew how to mix and blend healing potions. As time went on, separate apothecary shops were started. Huthmacher's was in a little building on the corner of Hibben and Church Streets. He advertised, using a picture of Fort Sumter, a healing ointment which he manufactured.

Other druggists had their small shops in various places in the Village. When Dr. Wacker arrived, his drug store was in the business district across Pitt Street from the Academy. His customers were soon aware of his willingness to go fishing. Life was not too structured in the days before the middle of this century.

Four
Churches and Cemeteries

Carolina was an English colony begun in 1670. The 1706 Church Act divided the low country into ten areas called parishes which combined the duties of church and state. Christ Church Parish included the area bounded by the Wando River, Charleston harbor, the Atlantic Ocean, and Awendaw Creek. The parish church, Christ Church (shown here c. 1900), was some 6 miles from the harbor. It was built in 1708.

In 1696 a group of New Englanders settled in what became Christ Church Parish near Awendaw Creek. They were Congregationalists; by 1699 a minister had been called. Soon Presbyterian ministers served Wappetaw Church.

It became customary for planters to leave their plantations in the summer for the healthier climate along the coast. With their families situated in summer cottages, they would go back and forth to oversee the fields. These planters founded the churches in the Village.

The first record of a church building in what is now Mount Pleasant was a newspaper account in 1827 which stated a Village church was to be constructed.

Letters written by John Leighton Wilson in the summer of 1830 indicate a religious revival was taking place in the Village. He later became an outstanding Presbyterian minister.

This private residence, at 226 Bennett Street, was probably the Mount Pleasant Presbyterian Church, as recent renovations showed the center rooms to be quite old. Since the population of the area along the harbor was sparse, it is possible that the Village church mentioned in the newspaper account served several denominations. Times for services when ministers were available could well have been alternated, as was the custom in later years.

Even after the present Mount Pleasant Presbyterian Church was built in 1853, the congregation was quite small, and visiting preachers provided spiritual guidance. In 1870 it was accepted by the Charleston Presbytery as a Presbyterian church. At various times, this building, at the corner of Hibben and Church Streets in Lucasville, was shared with the Methodist and Lutheran congregations. Although it was used as a hospital during the war, the gashes in the posts supporting the balcony are just the height of a pew seat, much too low for nursing care, and are all on the same side, which discredits the idea they were used for stretchers, as tradition says.

Episcopalians living in the Village found a need to have a place of worship closer than Christ Church, some 6 miles away. By 1835 they had completed a chapel on the corner lot at Whilden and Venning Streets. Records show they paid $250 for the lot.

The chapel was soon outgrown and in 1857 the present brown frame St. Andrew's Episcopal Church was completed in the Gothic Revival style, designed by Edward Brickell White, who also did Grace Episcopal and the Huguenot churches in Charleston. Since most of the villagers refugeed upstate, the chapel was closed during the war. When it reopened in 1866 it was the only church open in the Village; even a Baptist served on the vestry. It separated from Christ Church in 1915 and received full parish status in 1954.

The choir of St. Andrew's is shown here in the early 1920s before they became a vested choir. Apparently it was a festive occasion—the church is quite decorated, and the ladies are in their Easter finery.

Not only was Adam Bennett the sexton; he pumped the organ to supply the air necessary for the pipes to sound when the organist played the keys. He would have operated a long handle up and down forcing air into the bellows.

Methodist Societies were organized in the area around 1799, but it was not until the 1830s that a building was erected on the corner lot of Hibben and Bennett Streets. Used as a hospital during the war, it was taken down in 1869 because of its condition. The Presbyterians shared their sanctuary until the present Eastlake-style Hibben United Methodist Church was constructed around the turn of the century. When rapid growth necessitated a move, they carried the Hibben name to their new property on Coleman Boulevard. The Seventh Day Adventists bought the old church and Sunday school building.

The German families settling in Mount Pleasant were Lutherans. For several years they held services in the Presbyterian church, then the ten families decided to build their own church. In 1884 they did so, in five months, and called it St. Paul's. Pastors from Charleston served the little congregation. Their first resident pastor came in 1927.

In 1898 Frank Muench was successful in getting the Lutheran Theological Southern Seminary moved from Newberry to the vacant courthouse building. A two-story frame refectory on Carr Street adjacent to the courthouse was provided for the students.

Professor Muench and the other faculty members lived in the brick house at 217 Bennett Street, which was enlarged to its present size at this time with the addition of the rear wing. When the student body outgrew the facilities, the seminary was moved to Columbia, SC, in 1911, where it remains.

Baptists originally had to travel to Charleston to attend church, but around 1871 they began worshipping in a building on Patjens Lane until it burned about 1875. In 1919 they purchased the old Berkeley County Courthouse, which had previously been used for the Lutheran Seminary, and converted it into the First Baptist Church of Mount Pleasant. Renovations such as outside stairs leading into the sanctuary made the courthouse more appropriate for church use. In 1964 their new sanctuary on McCants Drive was dedicated.

Mass was said in the homes of Catholic families because of the difficulty in getting to Sullivan's Island to attend Stella Maris Church. Pastors from there served those in Mount Pleasant. Around 1920 a small frame building was erected at 735 Pitt Street. It was known as Sacred Heart Chapel. About 1935, services were discontinued when the bridge to the island was opened. Today Christ Our King Church serves the area.

In the part of Mount Pleasant bordering Greenwich Common three Black churches, one Baptist, one Methodist, and one Presbyterian, were begun during Reconstruction. The Methodist, Friendship A.M.E., continues as the most active. It is just outside the National Register Historic District.

Walter ("Cheese") Porcher was indeed a "Community institution," as Reverend Johnson said at his funeral in 1994 at Friendship Church. A connection with the Village of yesteryear died with "Cheese." He began working about 1920 at Mr. LeGrand King's grocery store on Church Street and continued with the Colemans. He knew everyone and everyone knew him. Not only did he deliver groceries, he sometimes put them up for the customer. At his funeral both black and white friends came to pay tribute to the passing of this citizen. Mount Pleasant has been fortunate to have had many like him: church sextons, town marshall Edmund Jenkins, Village blacksmith Peter Simmons, shipbuilders, handymen, vegetable and seafood peddlers, and midwives. The list goes on with teachers and morticians.

In Christ Church Parish there are family burying grounds on private property, some called by the family name, others by the location. Other graveyards are associated with a nearby church. Although outside the National Register district, the large cemetery on McCants Avenue should be mentioned. An 1883 ordinance established the Ocean Grove Cemetery on Division and Boundary Streets (now McCants and Simmons). The area was to be divided between the races with Hallelujah Lane separating it. In 1889 the Lutheran congregation purchased the part now known as the Lutheran Cemetery, although people of all faiths are buried there.

The Confederate Cemetery (pictured here) is within the historic district. Located on Carr Street, there are tombstones that predate the war by many years. An old plat shows this area on Greenwich Common to be a cemetery which extends through to Royall Avenue. The Confederate Memorial Association oversees the cemetery, and the Town maintains the grounds.

Names on this tall slender monument honor the Confederate veterans from this area. Near the rounded marker lie some twenty-five who died in the hospital in the Presbyterian church. They were reinterred when excavation for the courthouse uncovered the remains. A custom from many years ago of decorating the graves with flags and flowers is continued every year on May 10. When the Academy was on Pitt Street the whole school was involved in this observance; afterward they had a holiday.

Both monuments pictured here are listed in the Smithsonians S.O.S. project—Save Outdoor Sculptures.

The massive War of 1812 Monument is 5 feet square and 12 feet tall. It is the only one known to honor these soldiers of long ago in the southeast. In 1970 the United States Daughters of 1812, South Carolina Society, erected the Archives and History historical marker which reads: "War of 1812 Encampment. The 1812 monument in this cemetery originally marked a burial plot of the Third Regiment of State troops. The soldiers who were buried there apparently died from disease while stationed at Haddrell's Point. Before the Civil War the monument is said to have stood at the corner of Pitt and King Streets. It was moved to this Confederate cemetery for protection from vandalism." The other side reads "On June 18, 1812, the United States declared war against Great Britain. One of the first units to be mustered into service was the Third Regiment of South Carolina Militia, which was stationed at Haddrell's Point, west of here, to aid in the defense of Charleston harbor. Their barracks stood within the present town limits of Mount Pleasant and they were equipped with State funds."

Five
Education in the Village

The Mount Pleasant Academy was incorporated by the General Assembly of the state on December 19, 1809. A school probably existed before that date although it was customary for families on plantations to hire a tutor for all the children. Aaron W. Leland was the tutor in James Hibben's family, and married James' oldest daughter Eliza. Aaron became headmaster of the Academy in 1809, and taught the classical department, while another teacher taught English. A third teacher, who taught French, was eventually added to the staff.

The site of the first school building is unknown. Later the school may have been located at 226 Bennett, the Village church; at other times it was housed in buildings at the intersection of Hibben and Coleman, at the corner of Bennett and Venning, and at the courthouse.

This house at 140 Hibben Street, constructed for the school, was first composed of two rooms, and later three. Near the corner of Hibben and Bennett Streets, it was built on part of the Methodist church lot and was used until 1908. Today, with alterations, it is a residence.

Students of the Academy in 1888 are pictured in these faded photographs. The headmaster at this time was Robert V. Royall, shown at the top left. The house at 140 Hibben would have been the schoolhouse.

Younger pupils appear in this picture. The teacher is not named. It would have been a two-teacher school at this time. When it returned from the courthouse, there were probably three rooms.

A composition by a fourteen-year-old student written as a school assignment described his response to this awesome event. Several other compositions have survived that he wrote for class assignments. He became a physician like his father.

THE CHARLESTON EARTHQUAKE

It will be many years before the memory of the earthquake on the night of August 31st [1886] will be erased from the memory of the people of Charleston.

It was a time of terrible suspense for no one was not to know at what time you would be swallowed up by the earth, and also you were in great danger of falling walls and tumbling chimneys.

We, the people of Mt. Pleasant, I think felt the Shocks, nearly, if not as bad as the people of Charleston.

The people all over the United States were very generous, a day or so after the first great Shocks a golden tide of money began pouring into Charleston, and in a few weeks many thousands of dollars had come in, if it had not been for this generosity on the part of the people, I do not know how the city would have been built up again, but it is now more beautiful than before.

Composition of J.P. DuPré
Mt. Pleasant
So. Ca.

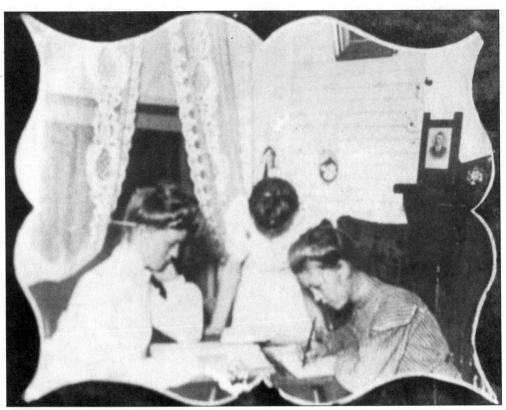

Homework keeps these sisters busy in the early 1900s. The photograph of the "three little maids from school" is rather remarkable because it was taken indoors at night.

This young lady graduate in 1901 from Memminger Normal School looks quite self assured, for high school boys went to Charleston High, and girls went to Memminger in Charleston. A later writer captioned this picture "and some day women will have careers too, just like men. There are lady typewriters already . . . Some day they may work on Broad Street . . . Some day they may even vote."

The Academy, built on the corner of Venning and Pitt Streets in 1908, filled the need for more than the three rooms on Hibben Street. The town had grown and there were more pupils to be taught. This building was used until 1938 by the grammar school. After that a high school was housed here for some years.

The first grade class of 1915 at the Mount Pleasant Academy is pictured. The twenty who were at school that day are seated informally outdoors, obviously facing the sun.

The first grade class of 1924–25 is lined up by the side of the Academy wearing their winter coats. The boys and the girls are about the same height. Although it is ten years later, there are still only twenty in the class.

The fifth grade class of 1924–25 standing by the side of the school building numbers fifteen. The girls are noticeably taller than the boys at this age.

The pupils and faculty of the Academy marched the three blocks from the school to the future site of the Academy on Boundary Street (now Simmons and Coleman) on President Washington's 200th birthday, February 22, 1932. The program included an opening prayer, the singing of "America," and the reading of extracts from a letter written by Washington and a tribute to him by another president. Each grade and the faculty planted a tree in a particular location while the band from Fort Moultrie played. Then they sang the "Star Spangled Banner" and the benediction was pronounced.

The six members of the faculty and the principal are flanked by the flag bearers, who are girls from an upper class. According to the pictures of the seven classes, the school enrollment at this time was about 185.

The third graders and their teacher are seated around a tree that has just been planted. It is "their" tree since each class had a designated site for a tree. The trees would do some growing before the new school was completed six years later.

The new building was completed in 1938. The sturdy two-story school was ready for its pupils, seven teachers, and principal. The wings would be added at a later time as the population grew. The Parent-Teacher Association published *Mount Pleasant's Famous Recipes* in 1938. Besides recipes it contained advertisements and a professional directory. The editor included this: "We may live without music, poetry and books, But civilized man cannot live without cooks."

Cornelia Hancock (pictured here), a former Civil War nurse, came to Mount Pleasant in 1866 for the purpose of starting a school for black children in the name of the Friends Association for the Aid and Elevation of the Freedmen of Philadelphia. In 1878 Miss Abby Munro succeeded Miss Hancock as principal, a position she kept for thirty-seven years.

The Presbyterian church was used by Miss Hancock for a few months. During the war a shell had exploded, making holes in the roof. When she started her school, fires were built on sand on the floor to keep warm; smoke escaped through holes in the roof. Without blackboards or chalk, she used charcoal to write on the columns. Necessity is the mother of invention.

The Friends Association rented 217 Bennett Street for the school, after it had been in the church for some six months. Here was space for the classrooms and for the teachers to live. The school stayed here for two years until a brick building was constructed on the corner of King and Royall Avenue in 1868, paid for by the Freedman's Bureau. The 1886 Earthquake destroyed this building.

Laing School was named for Henry Laing, treasurer of the Friends Association. The frame building constructed after the earthquake, was used until 1953. It was demolished and a playground is located on the site. After the Quakers had ended their support in 1940, it became the first accredited black school in the South Carolina School System. The name is continued by the Middle School on Highway 17. The 1926 60th Anniversary booklet stated there were 350 students and a thriving Parent-Teacher Association. The curriculum included academic subjects and industrial training—which included cooking, sewing, cobbling, and manual training. The influence of the school in the community was certainly a positive one.

Six
Activities on Shem Creek

Shem Creek, a boundary of the historic district, has played an important part in the life of the Village from the beginning of the little settlement on the Ferry Tract in the eighteenth century. It was used as a means of transportation, as a source of seafood as well as recreation, and it provided employment for local workers through the building and repairing of boats. As a tidal tributary it provided a quiet safe anchorage for small boats.

In Colonial days the government controlled ferry operation by granting charters. There were ferries in several locations in Christ Church Parish. Granite markers along the primitive roads told the traveler the distance to the ferry. Some still exist.

Hibben's ferry connected the Village with Charleston. Although a Loyalist during the Revolution, his property was later returned. Old plats that show shipbuilding on Shem Creek indicate the ferry dock was just off Haddrell Street at the foot of Wharf Street which was originally in the center of the Boatyard housing development. Mills *Atlas of 1825* shows the road ending at the creek not the harbor.

George Washington as President visited all the states. His Southern tour brought him to South Carolina in May 1791. After breakfasting at Snee Farm, he rode to Haddrell's Point, Shem Creek. His aide, John Trumbull, who later became a famous artist, made sketches here showing Charleston in the background. This portrait hanging in Charleston City Hall was painted later from them. For the trip to Charleston thirteen captains of ships in port manned the oars of the barge taking him across. Other boats and barges accompanied the entourage to the city where he was entertained most elegantly for a week before he proceeded on his journey. The picture from the City Hall Collection is used with permission.

Shem Creek was the site of industry as well as transportation. Jonathan Lucas bought Jonathan Scott's Greenwich Mill property on the creek in 1793. He rebuilt the mill and installed equipment which gave it the capability of being a sawmill as well as processing rice. It was water powered. Traces of the holding ponds can still be found in Shem Creek at low tide.

Jonathan Lucas from England became one of the big landowners in the Village. In addition to the property on Shem Creek, he bought two blocks bounded by Pitt, Royall, and Bank to McCants in 1803. Jonathan died in 1821. The rice mills he had built throughout the coastal area made the growing of rice a very profitable crop.

William Lucas, Jonathan's son, was also a large landowner. Trenholm and Holmes developed part of his property as Lucasville in the 1850s, which was incorporated into the Town in 1872. It also included a common area which bordered Shem Creek to be used by all the owners. As the war was drawing to a close and occupation was imminent, the mill and the house were burned to keep them from falling into enemy hands. Squire Tew described the tragic events of the federal occupation in February 1865 in a letter to his daughter then in Florida.

Diamondback terrapins were shipped from the creek to the Waldorf Astoria Hotel in New York to be made into terrapin soup. Boys caught them and sold them to Robert Magwood at the boatyard where they were kept in holding pens in the water until shipment, via the Clyde Lines. A measuring device checked the "cooter's" size. A competition, with the prize an original painting by ornithologist-artist Edward von S. Dingle, produced the winning costume, literally a man-sized terrapin.

This view of Shem Creek looking from the harbor toward the bridge shows a variety of craft tied up to the docks on the town side. Townspeople kept their boats on the creek. It was still quiet—the day of the big trawlers had not come, nor had the many restaurants that line the shore today.

This packing shed on Shem Creek was at the end of a causeway where produce from the fields was brought, put aboard freight boats, and taken to Charleston. Much of it was then shipped to northern markets. Truck crops were grown with bountiful harvests of asparagus, beans, and tomatoes.

Skipper was the only shrimp trawler operating out of Shem Creek in 1930, according to its captain, W.C. (Bill) Magwood. Built in 1908 at the E.O. Hall Boatyard, *Skipper* was bought in 1923 by Captain Bill and used as a freight boat until the opening of the Cooper River Bridge put the freight boats out of business. Portuguese shrimpers had arrived in the Charleston area in the 1920s. They advised him on the conversion, which took four months. As many as ninety trawlers operated out of Shem Creek during the heyday of shrimping.

Boat building and repair have been industries on the creek since early times. Plats indicate locations of facilities on a canal leading into the creek. In 1895 Captain Robert Magwood bought the property and leased part of it to the E.O. Hall Boatyard. Hall built the first racing sailboat, the *Nell*, about 1912. "Miss Susie" (Magwood) Freeman was another longtime owner. In 1921 the Mount Pleasant Boat Building Company, Inc., continued the operation until it closed some sixty years later. There were many fine artisans who worked there. Charlie North's sixty-seven years there began with Ned Hall and ended in 1964 with the Darbys.

E.O. Hall's home still stands on Bennett Street. Mr. "Ned" not only had a fine boatyard on Shem Creek, he was interested in sailing. He served on the executive committee of the newly formed Sea Island Yacht Club in 1910, and was instrumental in the founding of the Mount Pleasant club in 1913 in response to a call from Thomas J. Hamlin.

Seven
Ferries, Trolleys, and Buses

In this day of automobile travel it is hard to imagine how important ferry service was to the Village before there were bridges. Several companies have existed since Andrew Hibben's in 1770. Boats were transferred from one company to its successor. They carried thousands of passengers to work and to school in the city, and brought tourists to recreational places east of the Cooper.

In the leisurely twenty-minute trip passengers got to know each other. Business was transacted on the way. If notified ahead of time, schedules could be adjusted for particular events. Their bells and engines were a part of the Village sounds with an identity all their own.

The Ferry Street ferry began about 1847, when Jugnot and Hilliard, as the Mount Pleasant Ferry Company, opened Ferry Street and constructed a ferry house and wharf on the front beach. Some of their boats had been used on Shem Creek by Hibben. The *Hibben* and the *Coffee* were impressed for Confederate services but later returned to the company. The *Hibben*'s capacity was four hundred. Other boats included the *Mount Pleasant*, the *Massasoit*, and the *Governor Aiken*. They took people on excursions as well as their regular routes.

The *Sappho* and the *Pocosin* were "one enders," which meant they had to turn around to make the return trip. The *Sappho* was in service fifty years, from 1876 to 1926. In 1898, when the Ferry Street ferry house burned, her steam pumps helped subdue the flames.

The Omnibus was a stagecoach operated by Henry McNeill which met every ferry. It was pulled by two horses. The fare was 10¢ and on rainy days business was good. His headquarters was on Church Street near Hibben where he ran a livery stable as well. He had the first telephone in the Village, which he generously shared. His descendants are outstanding African-American families in Mount Pleasant.

The Hibben Street ferry was the next ferry company. It operated at the foot of Hibben Street on the front beach. The similarity of names certainly makes for confusion. The Hibben Street site was chosen in 1898 by Dr. J.L. Lawrence and associates, whose plan included developing Long Island, which they renamed the Isle of Palms, as a resort. They had ferries to bring tourists across the harbor, and trolleys to take them on to the island. Trains brought them to Charleston in response to advertisements. The ferry wharf can be seen in the background of the picture.

The *Lawrence* and the *Commodore Perry*, both "double enders," with a pilot house at both ends, joined the *Sappho* and *Pocosin* ferries in Dr. Lawrence's comprehensive project. The company was named the Charleston and Seashore Railroad Co. His resort at the Isle of Palms included a pavilion, Ferris wheel, carousel, and other attractions as well as the beach. One Fourth of July attracted five thousand visitors. (Both images on this page are from the 1964 history of the SCE&G Co.)

The trolleys met the ferries on the Hibben Street wharf. On holidays the ferries ran continuously and passengers raced to get a seat on the trolley. The long lines of trolley cars stretched for blocks. They were powered by Direct Current (D.C.) generators. Passengers were taken through Mount Pleasant across Sullivan's Island to the Isle of Palms. Stops were called stations; Sullivan's Island still uses that designation instead of street names. Trestles were constructed over the Cove and Breach Inlets for the trolleys. In Mount Pleasant the trestle was at the end of Pitt Street. Eventually a bridge was built to include cars. Now it is used by fishermen and birdwatchers and called the "old bridge."

The car barn housed the trolley cars when they were not in use. It filled the block at the intersection of Hibben and Whilden Streets. When no longer needed for trolley cars, it was used as a cannery.

The huge tank was no longer needed after the car barn was dismantled. Lawrence's project had come to an end because of various circumstances. Several smaller operations continued for some years. The Hog Island Ferry operated for about five years beginning in 1924 from a point of land on the harbor near Hog Island at the foot of the Cooper River Bridge. The Cooper River Ferry Commission operated the *Palmetto* and the *Lawrence*. The wharf was accessible by a paved causeway. A bridge had now been built over Shem Creek. The opening of the Grace Memorial Bridge over the Cooper River foreshadowed the demise of the ferry system.

The *Nancemond* and the *Mary C. Moorehead* were operated by Captain Shain Baitry from the end of Hibben Street for some nine years from 1930. They carried cars as well as people. The long wharf and ferry house at the foot of Hibben Street were destroyed by fire.

The *Cornwallis* and its twin the *Pelican* were operated by Captain Baitry out of Shem Creek; they carried both cars and people. The *Water Lily*, a converted yacht, carried only people. President Grover Cleveland was taken on the *Water Lily* from Charleston when on his way to the Santee Gun Club, of which he was a member. In time the *Palmetto* was sold and went to Brazil. The *Lawrence* was made into a barge used by the Guilds Towing Company. The *Pocosin* ended her days in the marsh near the Shem Creek Bridge; the *Sappho* in the Ashley River marsh. The ferry era had ended.

In 1917 the United States Navy had a rifle range just east of Mount Pleasant. One hundred acres of land was leased from George Goblet, and facilities were constructed for six hundred men. Thousands were trained here because groups only stayed for two weeks. It was also used by Citadel Cadets, the Coast Guard, and the U.S. Regulars from Fort Moultrie. To get from the Ferry out to the rifle range, the sailors were taken by a bus operated by Mr. Fred Tiencken.

When sailors arrived in Mount Pleasant they had no idea where they were and walked all around. Mr. Tiencken's daughter photographed this sailor and a young lady on roller skates across the street from her house as they sat on the wall in front of 217 Bennett Street.

Eight
Children

Several different types of pictures form the first section. There is the early daguerrotype and tintype as well as a picture of a glass negative. Carte de Visites (CDVs) made in a portrait studio were quite popular in the latter part of the last century. Large albums on tables in parlors held these pictures that were designed to fit in the pages in the album.

The "Joys of Childhood" section follows the more formal studio portraits. A more informal America was emerging by the turn of the century.

Lizzie (b. 1852) and Robbie (b. 1854) were the two oldest children of Dr. and Mrs. E.M. Royall. Lizzie married Thomas J. Hamlin, a planter; Robbie married Sallie DuPré and became a teacher and mayor of the town.

The uniform of this confederate soldier dates the daguerrotype. Probably expensive, these images were usually encased in a small album-like case. Sometimes it was leather, sometimes velvet.

Sallie DuPré (b. 1857) would have had to sit very still for this picture, which is a glass negative, about an inch square. It was wrapped in black paper when it was recently rediscovered. She was a niece of the doctor.

The young man who posed for this tintype was attracted by something that kept his attention focused. A tintype or ferrotype is a positive photograph made directly on an iron plate which had been varnished with a thin sensitized film. With age, it flakes off.

A young lady, whose name we do not know, sits demurely for the camera. The framing around the glass was usually gold with intricate designs.

The little lass in this small daguerrotype wears a locket around her neck. This type of photograph was invented by the Frenchman Louis Daguerre about 1839.

Three brothers born during and just after the war pose c. 1869 for the photographer, who is probably draped under a black cloth behind his large camera. The youngest had his hand behind his back because he had an orange. Children suffered the most during the deprivations of war and reconstruction. Yet one of these lads became a minister and the other a lawyer.

The doctor's daughter (b. 1878) holds her doll. They are both dressed in styles befitting adults.

Three brothers pose at the photographer's studio in Charleston. Descendants of the original Vennings, these boys stayed in the Village as adults and became good citizens. The photographer, W.B. Austin had the Van Dyke agency.

Two brothers dressed alike look solemnly at the camera. Both are wearing suits with fancy collars, and high-top shoes. The carte-de-visite was a Victorian memento shared with friends and relatives. Clarke's Studio was on King Street in Charleston. Large photograph albums had a prominent place in Victorian living rooms. Usually with a hard cover, they had leaves with holes of different sizes for the CDVs to be inserted.

The young man resplendent in his uniform with many buttons is in school. One does not know if this was a picture for a school annual, or just because his mother wanted a picture.

Three little sisters visit Clarke's Portrait Gallery on King Street. Their picture was shared with many aunts, uncles, and cousins. Many photographers had their studios on King Street.

The Pickens sisters pose with props at the studio. Austin advertised he was a Van Dyke Studio, and would keep negatives. Possibly the older sister had had typhoid; her hair is just growing back.

Three young gentlemen at the photographers look so mature with their hats and suits. The coat is almost overcoat length. The two at right and center are brothers.

Mary, holding her doll, stands in front of an elaborate prop at the photographer's studio. She was to be in a wedding. Dowling Studio in Charleston made this CDV in 1902.

A brother and sister visit the photographers in 1907. Imagine getting two youngsters to the city by ferry, and have them look so immaculate for their picture to be made. The sailor suit foreshadowed the young man's career in the Navy during World War II.

Dressed in a long dress in what is perhaps her first picture, this youngster was posed against the dark drape of Clark's Studio in 1903.

This is what the well-dressed baby wore in 1917. Caps kept the head warm. The little jacket, called a sacque, covered her shoulders.

"Mister White" greeted visitors at Christmas for many years at the Hibben House. The snowman was made of cotton. While neither child nor toy, he seems to divide the earlier pictures and the later ones.

The "Joys of Childhood" are portrayed in the series of pictures that follows. The rabbit on the bench by the baby indicates it was Easter. Though materials may change, animals have been toys for youngsters for years and years; in fact they may even take precedence over dolls.

Wagons were favorite toys. "Jackie" isn't too happy to be pulled around in it by his little master. Play clothes—rompers and a straw hat—and probably bare feet, made the summer of 1919 fun.

A teddy bear makes a good companion for this youngster and his wagon. Did you know they were named for President Theodore (Teddy) Roosevelt?

Girls played with wagons too. This 1912 photograph shows a fancy model wagon and a young lass, whose hat brim shades her face from the sun's rays.

Three playmates sit in a wagon which appears to be made of metal. They are in front of the school on Pitt Street. The year is 1930.

These two brothers are surrounded by their animals. A dog is on the left, a cat in the center, and rabbits in the wagon. It is the winter of 1918.

A baby toddles around as her big sister looks on, 1919. Rompers were worn by both girls and boys. Big sister has on her Sunday dress, complete with black stockings.

The two brothers on the horse are in the street by the Methodist church, c. 1922. The trolley tracks on Hibben Street made a sharp right onto Church Street and then into Pitt.

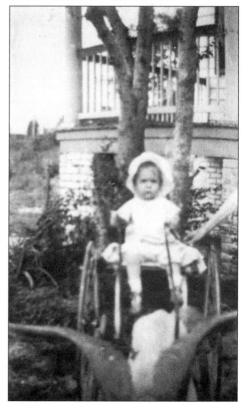

The goat almost walked out of the picture as it pulled the cart carrying the young rider. An adult's arm is visible steadying her.

87

This young miss enjoys the porch of her house as she takes her animals for a ride about 1910.

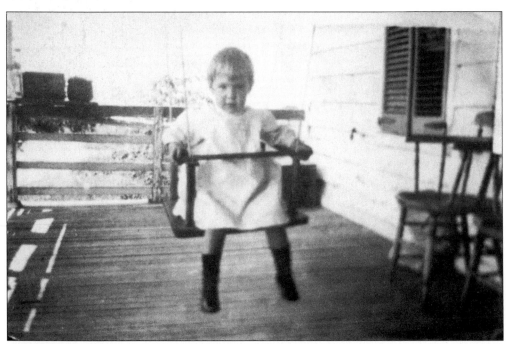

A swing on Grandma's porch was quite safe for the toddler.

Two friends at the garden gate have a talk. One, with his bookbag over his shoulder, is off to school. The year is about 1918.

Three children and four chairs in a row are in front of Grandma's house. A chair was a favorite Christmas present for a child. The small size made it special.

Dressed in overalls and a straw hat, this little farmer is ready to work. The year is about 1920.

These three cousins, who lived in adjoining houses, have a special toy—a chick on a stick. One might guess it is Easter.

Chickens were owned by everyone. What could be nicer than having soft baby chicks to play with?

A flock of chickens in the back yard eagerly peck grain that has been given to them by the child in the winter coat and cap.

Livestock in the Village was not at all unusual. There were no laws prohibiting it. Small buildings housed the animals.

"Daisy" the cow grazes contentedly staked out on a vacant lot. Bales of hay were brought over on the ferry and the trolley dropped them off at the proper house.

Nine
Recreation

Recreation and entertainment took many forms in this era. Water-related activities were certainly among the most popular things for young people to do. Traveling shows provided a peek at the outside world. A day in the country was fun; so was the simple pleasure of eating watermelon. Children loved birthday parties as well as playing in a playhouse. The beach was always beckoning, and a trip to the mountains helped escape the heat. Beach parties were fun, and so was camping out.

Bull's Island was an interesting place to be, particularly when surrounded by your contemporaries. This trip occurred before 1900. Bull's was a barrier island, to the north of the Village. The chain of islands were indeed barriers protecting the mainland from storms. Few people lived on them. The Magwood family had close ties to Bull's as well as to Mount Pleasant. Susie had invited her friends to share the pleasures there. Needless to say, a chaperone was along.

Canoeing could be enjoyed in the harbor. Here mother and daughter share the joy of a quiet ride. The time is about 1912.

A row boat like this, with a pointed bow, square stern, and flat bottom, was sometimes referred to as a bateau. The tide comes in rapidly, so the ladies would not have to wait long before they are afloat. Sullivan's Island is in the background to the right.

A motor launch could carry many friends. The *Eula* is probably in the Stono River. Friendship and kinship existed between young people in Mount Pleasant and James Island, and there was much visiting back and forth.

Sailing was probably the favorite water-related activity. In Charleston harbor the tidal breeze was sure to make it a pleasant trip. It was fun to sail alone, or to compete in impromptu races even when there was no regatta.

Entertainment came to the Village in varying forms. Shorty Griffin and his combination (what it was composed of we are not told) promised a "Grand Entertainment" to be performed at the Court House July 3 and July 6, 1895. Admission was 10¢ and 15¢.

Gilbert Walden and his group performed at the Knights of Pythias Hall on February 7, 1901. The price had increased to 15¢ and 25¢. His playbill promised two hours of laughter and enjoyment: fine music, songs, flute, guitar, and banjo by John M. McCrary, and thrilling story telling, throwing the lariat, and fancy rifle shooting by Walden the noted cowboy orator! Medicine shows traveled through the area as late as the 1930s. They used a vacant lot on Ferry Street, where they gave their nightly pitch with loudspeakers blaring forth.

Sidesaddle was the way ladies rode. This beautiful horse seems pleased to carry two lovely young ladies. The log cut with two steps provided them a way to mount.

The small four-wheeled buggy was an ideal way to go for a drive. The horse seems quite ready to pull the little carriage.

A day in the country provided fun for the two couples and their dog. They appear to be hiding behind a hedgerow while their picture is taken by the other young gentleman.

Barbed wire presents no obstacle when two friends are nearby to hold the strands apart for the young lady. The photographer is the other girl. One might guess it is a Sunday afternoon since the boys are dressed in suits and hats. But note the straw the one on the left has in his mouth.

Birthday parties were always special occasions. Here, about 1920, cousins celebrated with the guest of honor (holding an American flag).

A 1930 celebration with the "birthday girl" (seated in the front row, third from the right) included twenty-five friends. Note the white socks and black patent Mary Jane shoes the young ladies wore.

Eating watermelon, these three young ladies look quite happy. Apparently the one on the left has already finished hers.

A playhouse is every little girl's dream. The next best is having a friend who has one if you don't. In the back yard of a house on Pitt Street, this playhouse was quite spacious.

The highway to the beaches was Pitt Street. The trolley car trestle was replaced by a bridge for cars. Eventually the tracks were taken up, and the roadway paved. When the trolleys were operating, Charlestonians moving to Sullivan's Island for the summer even took along the family cow! Times certainly have changed.

The Ferris wheel on the Isle of Palms was said to be the highest in the world. Other attractions made the trip quite a bargain—plus there was always the beach for swimming and sunning.

The pavilion at the Isle of Palms was a site of social activity. Name bands played for "hops." For the price of a round trip fare, 15¢, everything could be enjoyed. Sad to say, it was destroyed by fire.

The beach, with waving sea oats on the sand dunes, formed a lovely backdrop for the young lady so elegantly dressed in flowing white dress, gloves, and hat, the style of the day.

The Isle of Palms Hotel, dance hall, and pavilion brought hundreds of people to the island. Note the dozens of old automobiles.

Bathing suits have certainly changed in design from the styles worn by these prospective swimmers. Sunscreen had not been developed. Broad-brimmed hats protected complexions instead.

Shadows on the shifting sand seem to intrigue this tot. "I have a little shadow that goes in and out with me, and what can be the use of him is more than I can see." Stevenson was right.

A couple walks under the umbrella, though it is not raining. Their shadows betray their closeness.

Riding on the beach was not prohibited in the 1930s. The pharmacist and his friends are ready to launch the boat for a day's fishing. His daughter, sitting on the boat, was the "birthday girl" on p. 99.

A plane ride from the Isle of Palms was possible on certain occasions. Pilot Fred Dorset taught stunt flyer Beverly Howard.

Beach pajamas were all the rage in 1929. They were not necessarily worn at the beach. Canvas tennis shoes completed the outfit.

College classmates found the style comfortable and quite a relief from the "long blue line" of Winthrop College uniforms.

A train from Charleston was the means of getting to the mountains. Before the days of air conditioning, those who could went to the mountains of North Carolina during the hot, humid lowcountry summers. Some families moved there, with the father making the weekend trip from home. Here the old coal-burning steam locomotive has just taken on water from the elevated tank. Two engines were needed to pull the Saluda grade in the mountains.

These couples appear to be planning something. It is not clear what the significance of the empty water bucket is. They are at Melrose, near Hendersonville and Brevard, NC, a favorite vacation spot for people from Mount Pleasant.

Walking the log is what they were planning. Holding hands made it so much more secure as they precariously made their way.

Success! They made it all the way to the end of the fallen tree. Seated, they contemplate the rushing mountain stream beneath them. A question—where was the photographer?

Friends from Mount Pleasant and James Island enjoyed each other's company and got together whenever they could. One such outing, to Folly Island on July 17, 18, and 19, 1907, was documented both by pictures and narrative. Each account came separately from descendants of members of the camping expedition. The story is told within a framework of the Raven writing everything that the bird saw. Descriptive names were given each of the campers, such as "Love Sick" and "Beau Ideal." The story in abbreviated form follows: on Wednesday at evening with sunset colors on the wake the *Stono* dropped anchor on Folly. Large bundles of bedding, boxes, lumber, and utensils were offloaded onto the beach. Supper was le cafe with du pain et la buerre.

"Slip Father" was chief boss of the camp. He saw that every one was comfortable, and did "picket duty" when night fell.

Tents were improvised with canvas tops by the Captain. One was designated for the chaperone and the girls. After excursions on the beach, a search for a turtle, finally all is quiet. The Raven waxed poetic:

The roar of surf, with break and splash,
Are God's appointed creatures;
To waft soft, dreamy, soothing sounds,
To lull the sleeping "beachers."
The picket guard is e'en at rest,
The stars, each, act a lamp;
And Luna holds herself aloft,
To guard the sleeping Camp.

The beachers awoke at 5:30 on Thursday morning and were soon off for a dip in the ocean. Visitors came soon, first the fishermen, then a horse and rider—an island resident who joins their party.

Entertainment included a story begun by one and continued by others in turn, creating anything they choose, which is embellished as it proceeds with stories of feuds, romances, duels, and miracles.

More friends arrived aboard a launch just after sunset. They visited for an hour or so and everyone went to the beach where they found a turtle making her nest.

Friday morning brings a visit from those miserable little marsh sand flies. Oil of citronella is the lesser of the evils even though its odor is pervasive.

The time has come to depart. Camp is dismantled, but an interruption occurs when the fisherman lands a 7-foot shark.

The trip home is begun with the *Belle*, its fisherman and his catch attached to the side of the *Stono*. The Raven concludes her story with the hope of the jolly crowd that they may again meet for a stay on Folly Island.

Boating was a social event for which the ladies dressed in their best attire. Styles were quite feminine with lovely long skirts. Bouffant hairdos were covered with wide-brimmed hats to protect the fair complexions.

These young gentlemen, dressed in suits, ties, and hats, appear to be waving good-bye at the conclusion of a happy excursion. Although the boats may appear crudely made they were quite sturdy and safe.

Camping out in the country. For Village boys nothing could have been finer than a weekend in the country. After school was out, loading up the model A, then bumping down rutted unpaved roads to a place they termed "Kilmo" was the eagerly anticipated pleasure. This was a time of peace and tranquillity. World War II was not yet on the horizon.

Hunting and fishing were pleasures each in its own season. The dog seems to know about the special privilege extended him. He probably rode on the running board of the Ford.

A long-vacant plantation house, belonging to the family of some of the boys, provided housing with no domestic restrictions. Beds did not have to be made, nor floors swept.

A chimney still standing from a slave house of long ago made an excellent oyster roaster.

Oysters were to be had from the nearby creek. Care had to be taken that bare feet were not cut on the oyster shells along the shore.

A boat made gathering the succulent bivalves much easier along the sloping shore. It is said an Indian tribe lived along this beautiful creek. There is clay in various places that was used in making brick in later times. Palmettos from this plantation lined the streets of Mount Pleasant from the foot of the bridge to the Isle of Palms in 1929.

Food from the creek that divided the plantations was plentiful. Fishing or casting for shrimp produced more than enough for the boys to eat with what they had brought from the home pantry.

Two Isaac Waltons show their catch of the "one that did not get away." By suppertime they will be in the frying pan.

Ten
Growth Begins

The opening of the Cooper River Bridge in 1929 and the dedication of the Mount Pleasant Waterworks in 1935 marked the beginning of change for the little village. Then in 1937 they looked back on a century of incorporation and took a look toward the future.

On August 8. 9, and 10, 1929, the opening of the bridge connecting Mount Pleasant and Charleston and the dedication of the Charleston Airport was celebrated.

It took only three-and-one-half years from the contract to the completion of the bridge. It was of cantilever design, 2.5 miles long, and named in honor of a former mayor. It was a toll bridge until 1947.

Likened by some to a roller coaster, the curve between the two spans was necessary to cross both the Cooper River and Town Creek at right angles.

An advertisement said it was the connecting link in the wonderful north-south highways, the ocean highway and the sea-level route. It was considered one of the largest, most impressive, and most unusually constructed bridges in the world. The ad continued: "It promises a thrill every time you cross."

On Thursday there was a military parade, a naval parade, musical programs, and the official opening of the bridge with John P. Grace, president, Cooper River Bridge Incorporated, as master of ceremonies. Toll rates were suspended until 4 pm. That afternoon a 25-mile automobile race on the beach was run. The day concluded with music until 2 am at the pavilion.

Friday featured the historic floats parade that wound through Charleston, crossed the bridge to Mount Pleasant, and then returned to Marion Square in Charleston. Outboard motor races were held on the back beach of the Isle of Palms that afternoon, and a sparring exhibition took place there that evening. There were more musical programs at the pavilion from 9 pm until 2 am. Saturday's events took place at the airport.

The Christ Church Parish History Club prepared the list of historic spots beyond the Cooper River which was included in the dedication brochure. It could be said they were the first Chamber of Commerce for the area. These five ladies loved history and were intent on preserving it. They met every other week in a member's home, assigned topics for research, wrote papers—some were published in the *News and Courier*—and went on field trips. Flat tires were a usual accompaniment, but that didn't daunt them. They are seen here on the bridge before it was opened to traffic.

The insignia of the Parish History Club shows an adaptation of the engraving on an old ten shilling note, showing the Battle at Sullivan's Island, 1776. The club met for about ten years beginning in 1926. The minute book is a delight to read. The membership was composed of Mrs. William Whilden (Petrona Royall) McIver, Mrs. Ferdinand (Esther Royall) Gregorie, Mrs. F.H. Horlbeck, Mrs. Alex Moore, and Mrs. George F. Von Kolnitz.

MOUNT PLEASANT HISTORY . . .

To those who seek authentic information on the colorful history of Christ Church Parish and the town of Mount Pleasant . . .

the Parish History Club will gladly answer all inquiries . . .

Address

Parish History Club Of Christ Church Parish

Box 282, Mt. Pleasant, S. C.

This scene on Bennett Street from one of Patjens postcards shows electricity had come to the Village. It came from the city under the harbor. Occasionally a ship would drop anchor and cut the cable and the Village would be in darkness. In 1928 the South Carolina Power Company acquired the Mount Pleasant Lighting Company.

Telephone lines were strung along the edge of the marsh. Many changes occurred from the party lines of several subscribers with different rings to the present-day service by BellSouth.

The Village Water Supply. Along the coast the water table is near the surface of the earth; consequently, wells do not have to be very deep. A town well is known to have been on Venning Street near Pitt in Mount Pleasant Village. In 1895, an artesian well was bored at the southeast corner of Pitt and Morrison. The water was said to be quite healthy since it contained traces of sulphur and soda. A bucket and rope were used to draw water from the well in the yard of the home. The old oaken bucket of the song was sometimes made of cedar, a fragrant wood. Pitcher pumps were also used. Shaped like a pitcher the pump was fitted to the pipe that went down to the water level. A small amount of water primed it, and water flowed as the handle was pumped.

Windmills were sometimes used to draw water. Dependent on the wind to turn the blades of the wheel, the water was stored in an elevated tank. Tidal breezes were predictable wind sources. Cisterns, either in the yard or inside the house, were also utilized to store rainwater.

A waterworks system, a long awaited and much needed project, came into existence in 1935. In view of all the technical and legal aspects, two years seems a short time for it to have been accomplished. Three deep wells provided 160,000 gallons daily with electrically driven pumps. There was one 100,000-gallon elevated tank 160 feet above mean sea level, and a 300,000-gallon steel storage tank in case of a fire emergency or the failure of the deep well pumping mechanism.

The pumping station building housed pumps both electrically powered and gasoline driven for emergencies for fire service. There were twenty-one fire hydrants. Water mains extended 5.8 miles. The booklet published for the dedication on October 17, 1935, contained articles of economic and historical interest. Mayor Erckmann cited the opening of the Cooper River Bridge and the completion of the waterworks system as reasons for future growth and prosperity for the Town of Mount Pleasant.

A century of incorporation was observed in 1937 with a play involving some forty actors and musicians at the recently constructed Alhambra Hall. It has been said that to know where we are going, we have to know where we have been. Five scenes were photographed which illustrate the adage. In this one the citizens of the villages seek the incorporation of Mount Pleasant and Greenwich in 1837. The area is platted showing the streets, and noting structures there.

Mount Pleasant Academy is founded. The boast was made that it would be second to none. The headmaster is shown lecturing the pupils.

125

War clouds gather, secession is discussed, further events result in the firing of the first shot.

Women in war time have difficult decisions to make. The men are off to war. Adequate food is hard to get. Refugeeing upstate is necessary when fighting progresses to this area.

Mount Pleasant today is described in speeches by Mayor W.L. Erckmann, Charleston Mayor Burnet Maybank, and Judge F. VonKolnitz.

The audience that evening filled the hall. After the performance a barbeque dinner and dance completed the festivities.

The past and the future are represented by the burned ferry wharf and the bridge over the Cooper River. When the Village of Mount Pleasant was laid out in 1808 a boast was made that it would have a sawmill, gristmill, brickyards, broom and spoke and handle factories, fine churches, and an incorporated Academy second to none. All these predictions of the founding fathers certainly came true. They would rejoice to know that indeed they had created a village that has become a splendid town. One hundred years after the first villages were incorporated, the East Charleston County Development Board adopted a slogan, pertinent to the era: "Mount Pleasant, where highways, waterways, and power lines meet—the buckle of the vegetable belt." As the era of the Victorian Village drew to a close, the promise of future growth and development was assured.